The Dawn of Time

AUSTRALIAN ABORIGINAL MYTHS

Also by Ainslie Roberts and Charles P. Mountford
THE DREAMTIME

THE
DAWN OF TIME

AUSTRALIAN ABORIGINAL MYTHS
IN PAINTINGS BY **AINSLIE ROBERTS**
WITH TEXT BY **CHARLES P. MOUNTFORD**

Line Illustrations by Ainslie Roberts

RIGBY LIMITED

RIGBY LIMITED, ADELAIDE • SYDNEY
MELBOURNE • BRISBANE • PERTH
FIRST PUBLISHED 1969
REPRINTED OCTOBER 1969
REPRINTED NOVEMBER 1970
REPRINTED OCTOBER 1971
REPRINTED JULY 1972
COPYRIGHT © 1969 AINSLIE ROBERTS AND CHARLES P. MOUNTFORD
LIBRARY OF CONGRESS CATALOG CARD NUMBER 69-13308
NATIONAL LIBRARY OF AUSTRALIA CARD NUMBER & ISBN 0 85179 304 5
ALL RIGHTS RESERVED
WHOLLY SET UP AND DESIGNED IN AUSTRALIA
PRINTED IN HONG KONG

TO THE BROWN PEOPLE
who handed down these Dreamtime Myths

CONTENTS

THE
DAWN OF TIME

Carved
Ceremonial
Objects

THE AUSTRALIAN ABORIGINES ARE A UNIQUE PEOPLE.
We do not know their place of origin, nor are we certain when they
reached this continent, although recent archaeological research has
shown that it was over twenty thousand years ago.

They are exclusively a hunting and food-gathering race, collecting
their sustenance at the time and place as Nature provides. This task
begins each morning, and no-one can tell what the day will bring. Their
tools and weapons, made only from wood and stone, are the simplest
owned by any living community; nor do they use metal in any form.
The aborigines are a perfect example of stone-age men living in modern
times. Yet, in spite of this material poverty, the aborigines have a wide
range of cultural expressions that both enrich and vitalize their life,

and an extensive mythology that reveals their concept of the origin of the world about them. These myths are accepted as a record of absolute truth; an answer to all the questions that arise in the ceremonial and daily life of the people. The saying, "As it was done in the Dreamtime, so must it be done today," dominates all aspects of aboriginal behaviour.

The beliefs of the people are expressed in all phases of their aesthetic life; in the narratives of the story-teller, in the graphic arts, in the realms of music and in the dramatic rituals of the ceremonial grounds. It is by the outpourings of these rich, if simple, cultural expressions, that the deeds of the mighty heroes of creation times are perpetuated.

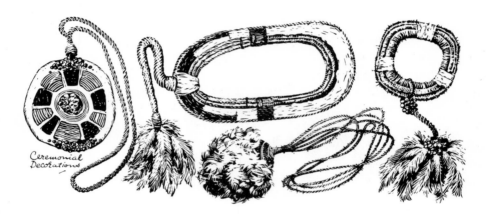

Ceremonial Decorations

The aboriginal story-tellers, although the least spectacular, are an important section of the community. Without any written form of communication, these story-tellers provide an invaluable means of passing on the laws of the tribe from one generation to the next.

It is also from the story-tellers and the older folk that the children first learn about the origin of the world in which they live, of the creatures they see, of the natural forces of wind and rain and of the stars above. Nevertheless, these little people do not receive any formal education as we know it. They appear to do just as they please, wandering around in small groups, searching for tid-bits of food, playing in the sands of the creek-beds, or sitting together chanting their childish songs. For the boys, education for their future has not yet begun.

But, one evening, the happy carefree life of one of the youths is completely shattered. He is hunted from the main camp, forbidden all contact with the women, and forced to live under the complete dominance of the gruff, unresponsive old men. These men, the sole repositories of tribal law and wisdom, will be the tutors of the initiate during his long and difficult road to manhood.

During the many years of his training, the youth, now treated as an outcast, lives in complete obedience to his elders, who teach him slowly, but none-the-less rigorously, the laws of his community, the relationship he bears to every member of it, and, as his education progresses, the secret myths and the rituals that reveal to him the inner mysteries of adult life.

There are several years of this harsh training before the initiate passes through rituals that admit him to full tribal status. Even then, it will be several more years before he will be sufficiently qualified to pass on to succeeding generations the store of knowledge he has accumulated.

Graphic art is used by the aborigines for many purposes; to beautify the objects they use from day to day and to express their mental images as visual symbols on the cave walls, on rock surfaces, and on sheets of bark. These art expressions can be divided into two main groups, the immovable, and the movable.

The immovable arts of cave paintings and rock markings are unequally distributed throughout Australia. There are no rock engravings along the south and south-western coasts, although they are, in simple forms, widely scattered throughout the rest of the continent. In the Hawkesbury River basin of New South Wales, and in north-western Australia, however, the forms are much more complex. Elaborate patterns were once cut in the trunks of trees and on the floor of the ceremonial grounds belonging to the now extinct Bora initiation ceremonies of eastern New South Wales. On the other hand, ground paintings associated with sacred totemic rituals and sand drawings, a means of instructing the initiates, are still living arts in central Australia.

The motifs employed in the cave paintings vary widely. Those in the south are simple in design, but toward the northern coasts this art, enriched by influences from the Indonesian and Melanesian Islands, becomes increasingly complex. In fact, the paintings in the caves of western Arnhem Land are, without doubt, the most beautiful in Australia.

In the realm of the movable art, the intricate patterns engraved on the shields, spear-throwers, and the inner surface of the skin rugs of Victoria, and those painted on the large wooden shields of Queensland in red, yellow, black and white, make these specimens of aboriginal craftsmanship objects of unusual beauty.

The aborigines of Arnhem Land once painted their mythical stories, and representations of creatures, on the insides of their bark huts during the enforced idleness of the wet season and, in more recent times, on sheets of bark for sale. Many of the earlier examples of these bark paintings conform in line, colour, and spacing of design elements to the same principles that characterise all good art, ancient or modern.

The red, yellow, black and white pigments used on the cave and bark paintings of Arnhem Land are obtained either from local deposits or by trade from neighbouring tribes. When required, these pigments are ground to a cream-like consistency on a rough stone and applied to the painting surface with simple brushes.

The brushes are of several forms: a narrow strip of bark, chewed at one end, for the broad lines, and a cylindrical stick about three-sixteenths of an inch in diameter for the dots. A third brush, requiring considerable skill in its use, made from a few fibres of palm leaf or from a small feather, is held delicately between finger and thumb and drawn away from the body. The colourful cross-hatched panels that characterise the art of Arnhem Land are all made with this type of brush.

The artists of this area employ several fixatives to hold the colour on the painting surface: the juice of a tree orchid, cut in halves and crushed slightly by chewing; the wax of the stingless bee, well mixed with water, and the white of the eggs of the sea-going turtle. The fixative is usually rubbed directly on the surface, although in some areas it is mixed with the pigments on the grinding stone.

Art is used more extensively than elsewhere in the colourful Pukamuni burial ceremonies of Melville Island. During these rituals, extending over many weeks, the face and body of everyone who takes

Ceremonial
Head Ornaments

part is painted in coloured ochres with the most grotesque patterns. At
the final ceremony, the mound of the grave, covered with painted bark
containers and finely carved spears, is surrounded by a circle of
elaborately carved and decorated poles.

Milling around this dramatic spectacle is a crowd of hysterical men
and women, chanting the high-pitched *amburu* song of mourning. The
last phase of the Melville Island burial ceremony is a sight without
parallel in aboriginal Australia.

Music is a fundamental and powerful urge in all people, especially
the non-literate. This is particularly true of the Australian aborigines
who, except for a simple wooden trumpet used by some tribes along the
northern coasts, have no musical instrument whatever, although a
pair of beating sticks is sometimes used to mark the rhythm of song and
dance. Yet this music, simple in form, permeates all aspects of aboriginal
life.

There are the soothing lullabies of the women to coax restless infants
and sick people to sleep; the simple refrains of the children as they sit
around their smoky fires, and songs of the traveller who, returning from
a journey, chants an episode in his experiences.

But the most vital musical expressions of the aborigines belong to the ceremonial grounds where the "lines" of songs, often made of a hundred and more verses, describe the journeys and exploits of one of the totemic heroes. These songs are chanted by the men, although on occasions the women sit unobtrusively in the background and beat their laps in time with the music and the dancing.

Music is also used for beneficent purposes. Some chants increase the supplies of fruit on the trees, some cause the animals to multiply, others create rain and the many daily needs. Music is, by its own right, a source of much enjoyment to the aborigines. To see the look of ecstatic pleasure on the faces of the men as they chant the apparently endless verses of a song cycle, or the satisfied expressions on the faces of the women when they beat time to the feet of the dancing men, is to realise how music is an integral part of the cultural life of these people.

Drama, a blending of both music and mime, is the most powerful and, at the same time, the most beautiful of all the aesthetic expressions. From childhood to old age, drama plays an important part in the life of every individual. It is present in the first ceremony of the youths as they perform one of their childish myths, their painted bodies gleaming like polished bronze in the early morning sunlight; in the dignified songs and rituals of the ceremonial ground, when the initiate receives the badge that admits him to tribal manhood, and in the ceremonies of death when, to the songs of mourning, the dancers mime the actions of the totemic creatures belonging to the dead.

Many of the evening rituals in the ceremonial grounds are spectacles of great beauty. The singers, dimly visible in the flickering light of the camp-fires, chant the songs to the rhythm of the beating sticks, while the actors, their bodies decorated with symbolic designs and conscious of nothing but their art and the ancient stories, mime, with extraordinary skill, an episode of the distant Dreamtime.

These vital performances in which the aborigines re-enact their mythical history are probably the simplest forms of drama, yet they resemble some of the great operas of our own culture in one important respect. Whereas Wagner has immortalised the mighty deeds of the gods and demi-gods of the ancient Nordic race, so the aborigines, by their age-old chants and strange rituals, have kept alive the epics of their own heroic past. But the functions of the two expressions are totally different.

To the people of our civilisation, a Nordic opera provides a pleasant evening of entertainment, a diversion from the daily tasks, but to the aborigines their ceremonies are the essence of the tribal history—vivid links between their past and their present.

The cultural expressions of the aborigines form a central core which, through the media of the story-teller, the artist, the singer and the actor, keeps alive the beliefs of the tribe, and at the same time provides the people with a wealth of creative pleasure that enriches their lives.

CHARLES P. MOUNTFORD

St. Peters, South Australia

THE FIRST SUNRISE

The Australian aborigines are deeply interested in the universe about them, the stars, the sky, and in particular, the earth itself. Out of this timeless interest has grown a rich heritage of myths and beliefs: the earth floats in the middle of a boundless ocean; it is a disc of limited size, moving in the sky just below the stars. And over the horizon is the land of the dead; a land with streams of running water, shady trees, ample food, and perpetual fine weather.

One ancient story describes how the sky was so close to the earth that it not only shut out all light, but forced everyone to crawl around in the darkness, collecting, with their bare hands, whatever they could find to eat.

But the magpies, one of the more intelligent birds, decided that, if they all worked together, they could raise the sky to make more room in which to move about. Slowly, with long sticks, the birds lifted the sky, resting it first on low, then on higher boulders, until everyone could stand upright.

As the magpies were struggling to lift the sky even higher above their camp, it suddenly split open, revealing the beauty of their first sunrise. Overjoyed with the light and warmth, the magpies burst into their melodious call and, as they sang, they saw the blanket of darkness break into fragments and drift away as clouds.

From those remote times until now, the magpies have always greeted the sunrise with their warbling song of incomparable beauty.

30″ x 48″ · *Mr and Mrs John A. Michell*

THE CREATION OF SPENCER GULF

Spencer Gulf, in South Australia, was once a valley filled with a line of fresh-water lagoons, stretching northwards for a hundred miles or more. Each lagoon was the exclusive territory of a species of water bird. One group belonged to the swans and the ducks, another to the grebes and the cormorants, still another to the water-hens, coots, and reed warblers. The trees belonged to the eagles, crows and parrots, while in the open country between the lagoons lived emus, curlews and mallee fowls. Further out were the animals, the dingoes and many kangaroo-like creatures, and in the thick grass by the waters were snakes, goannas and lizards.

For a long time all lived in harmony. But trouble started when the birds, because of their greater numbers, more beautiful appearance, and their ability to fly, felt so superior to the rest of creation that they prohibited the animals and reptiles from drinking at the lagoons. Thus began a long conflict in which many were killed, and large numbers of land-dwellers died of thirst.

In those days, the kangaroo was a man who grieved over the unnecessary fighting. Thinking over the situation, he finally decided that if an opening could be made in the southern isthmus, which in those days blocked the sea from entering the valley, the conflict would be ended by the flooding of the lagoons.

Now the kangaroo-man possessed the thigh bone of a mythical ancestor. With this bone, he had already performed many wonderful deeds. So he pointed the bone at the isthmus, which slowly split open. The sea poured through the opening, flooding the entire valley, so that the birds and the animals were forced to live together in peace.

27" x 36"   *Miss Marcella Reale*

THE WHISPERING BLUE BIRDS

The aborigines who live along the shores of the River Murray have left behind many interesting stories about the exploits and adventures of a tall powerful man, Nurunderi, who enlarged the river to its present size and created the natural features along its banks and the fish that live in its waters.

In this story, Nurunderi's two wives, who were sisters, had run away from him. He had pursued them in his simple wooden canoe, and while looking for them near the shores of Lake Alexandrina, he passed a point of land covered with a dense growth of reeds. This place was the home of a group of extremely shy people, who so feared Nurunderi that when they saw him coming they whispered to each other, "Stoop low as you walk, or he'll see you."

Although he heard them moving about, Nurunderi could not catch a glimpse of the little people, for as he moved in closer they pushed their way through the reeds and disappeared.

Annoyed by this behaviour, Nurunderi transformed these shy people into small birds, which still live on the shores of the lake. They always fly below, never above, the tops of the reeds and, like their forebears of old, chirp continuously as if whispering to each other.

27" x 36"   *Lieutenant-General Sir Edric and Lady Bastyan*

NURUNDERI'S FISHING NET

Nurunderi, unhappy because his wives were not with him, made another attempt to find them. Stepping across the mouth of the River Murray, which was then, as now, a maze of shifting sandbanks and turbulent waters, he travelled north-west until he came to a narrow inlet, Ratalang. Here is a natural fish trap, with a dense growth of sea-weed that almost closes the opening. During the Dreamtime, this sea-weed was a tree which Nurunderi had thrown into the water to drive the fish into his net. Later, the aborigines caught many fish in the same way.

Nurunderi made his camp on a headland, and cast his net in the shallow waters of a nearby beach. But, hearing his wives some distance away, he threw his net on a group of boulders and set off in pursuit. The dark-coloured pattern of his net can still be seen on the rocks.

Nurunderi soon came to Pultana, a wide bay on whose sands he saw the tracks of his wives. Annoyed at being unable to find their camp, he cast three spears into the sea, each of which turned into a rocky island. He then climbed to the summit of a rugged promontory from where he could see his wives should they be walking along the beach.

As the sun was hot and there were no trees, Nurunderi built himself a shade with three granite boulders, placing a fourth on top. The aborigines believe that this promontory was once the sleeping body of Nurunderi, with his head under that pile of rocks.

27″ x 36″   *Mrs B. J. Parsons*   23

THE TWO SISTERS

Nurunderi soon left his camp under the boulders and continued the search for his wives. He knew they were not far away for, though he could not find their tracks along the shore, he often heard their laughter as they swam in the breakers or chased each other through the shallow waters.

Nurunderi, wishing to create another island, climbed to the top of a high cliff to throw a spear into the sea. It was while standing on this point that he saw his two wives crossing over to Kangaroo Island, which in those remote times was separated from the mainland only by a line of partly submerged boulders. Their attempt to escape made Nurunderi so angry that, waiting until they were half way across, he roared with a voice of thunder, "Let the seas roll and destroy those who escape me."

Instantly, a large flood of water started to pour into the narrow strait. Wave after wave struck the women until they were swept from the boulders and carried out to sea. Terrified at their predicament, and the fury of the waters, the two women tried to swim back to the mainland but the current swiftly overcame them and they were drowned.

Their bodies were transformed into two islands in Backstairs Passage, known as the Pages, the larger being the elder sister and the smaller island being the younger one.

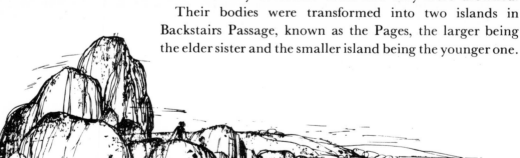

36″ x 45″   *Mr G. L. Parsons*

WILDU AND THE NORTH WIND

An old eagle, Wildu, and his two young kestrel wives, once lived in the rugged Flinders Ranges of South Australia. It was the duty of Wildu to train his nephews, a crow, Wakala, and a magpie, Kinita, in the rules and beliefs of the tribe. But the lives of the nephews were made so unbearable by the exacting demands of Wildu that they speared him. Screaming with pain, Wildu flew northwards where he died.

By their action Wakala and Kinita were released from the domination of their uncle, and given the opportunity of stealing his wives. But the kestrels, escaping their captors, went searching for their husband and, after a while, noticed a feather blowing along the ground.

Rising high in the air, the kestrels fluttered their wings, as kestrels still do, until they drew up such a violent storm of wind from the north that it tore many more feathers from Wildu's body. By tracing the feathers back to their source, the kestrels found their dead husband.

They spent many hours chanting songs of magic before they brought Wildu back to life. But when he heard that his nephews and their friends were holding a corroboree to celebrate his death, Wildu, flying into a violent rage shouted "I'll kill everybody in the world, none shall escape."

But the kindly kestrel women insisted that he must not kill in anger, but only as they did, when hungry. Finally Wildu agreed to spare the creatures, but he insisted that he would disfigure, though not kill, the crow and the magpie.

27" x 36"   *Dr and Mrs Howard W. Welch*   27

THE CAVE OF FIRE

The eagle, Wildu, furious with his nephews, soon made plans for revenge. From the summit of a high mountain, Wildu could see the birds and animals dancing to celebrate his death. The crow and the magpie stood out from the grey-coated animals, because, in those early days, both of those birds had glossy-white plumage.

Now Wildu, knowing of a cave in a group of boulders not far from the corroboree ground, estimated that a sudden squall of rain would drive all the performers into the cave for shelter. So the eagle asked his wives, the kestrels, to go into the air again and flap their wings, this time to draw up a heavy storm of rain from the south.

Everything happened as Wildu had planned. When the rain started to pour down, the performers rushed to the cave. The animals went in first, then the magpie, and finally the crow, their bodies almost blocking the entrance. This suited the purpose of the eagle very well. Quickly, he and his wives covered the opening with a huge pile of grass and dead branches, and set them on fire.

When the fire died away, it was found that the wallabies, bandicoots and other creatures had escaped unmarked. But the crow and the magpie were not so fortunate; the glossy plumage of the crow, who was nearest to the fire, was scorched completely black, while that of the magpie, being further from the fire, was scorched only in parts.

And, the aborigines explain, that is the reason why all the crows are black, and the magpies black and white.

27″ x 36″   *Mr and Mrs Nigel Morgan*

THE NIGHT-DWELLING SPIRITS

Throughout Australia, the aborigines believe in spirits who seek to injure or kill those who travel alone, particularly at night. These spirits assume many forms. In the deserts of Central Australia, the Mamu, a large spirit dingo, captures and eats the spirit of any child who wanders away from the light of its camp-fire. On Melville Island, the Mopaditis, the spirits of the newly-dead, try to steal the souls of living people to keep them as companions in their loneliness.

The aborigines on the rugged plateau of Arnhem Land are afraid of the Nadubi, a spirit people with barbed spines growing from their elbows and knees. A Nadubi will creep up to a solitary traveller and project a spine into his body. Sometimes a medicine man, by extracting the spine, can save the patient, but more often he dies.

On Groote Eylandt in the Gulf of Carpentaria, the aborigines dread the Gurumukas, tall, thin spirits with long projecting teeth. These spirits are particularly active on dark nights, and should one of them see an aboriginal walking by himself, it will bite him in the back of the neck. Unless the victim is able to call a medicine man immediately, he will die in great pain. However, as the Gurumuka attacks solitary people, and then only in the darkness, everyone is safe if he travels in company with others, or keeps within the light of his own camp-fire.

It is the duty of the medicine men, the only people who can see these malignant spirits, to hunt them away from the camp. But sometimes, when the medicine men are not sufficiently vigilant, or the spirits are too clever, a piteous death wail announces that some wanderer has met his fate.

27" x 36" *Mr and Mrs Ernest Just*   31

PIPINYAWARI, THE QUEEN FISH

A myth from northern Australia tells of a spear-throwing contest, and the creation of the first gum trees. When the people of Melville Island were assembled for the final burial rituals of their great creator, Purukupali, the fish-men arranged a contest to find out who could throw his spear the furthest.

Pipinyawari, their leader, proved to be the most skilled, for his spears always travelled further than any of the others. Later, the spears that were thrown became gum trees, the largest of them being the spear thrown by Pipinyawari. But in his effort to win, the leader injured his spine so badly that part of the vertebra was forced through the skin of his back.

At the conclusion of the burial rituals, it was the duty of Pipinyawari to pay the fish-men who had helped to carve and decorate the poles for the grave. But Pipinyawari did not do so, thus committing a breach of faith that so enraged his companions that they chased him through the bush to spear him. Trying to escape, Pipinyawari jumped into the sea, changing himself into a queen fish. But the other men, still infuriated, also changed themselves into fish and continued the chase.

On calm days, the aborigines often see Pipinyawari, still trying to escape his pursuers, rise out of the sea in a great curve, his broken spine now grown into a large dorsal fin.

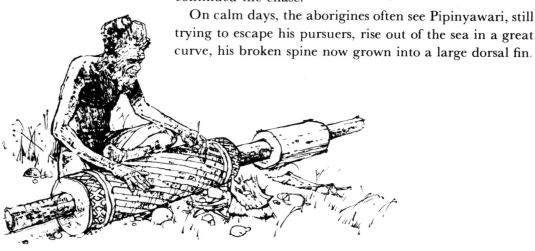

32

Tjinjawari and the first Gum Tree

Hinshi Roberts
1961

27" x 36"   *Mr Walter K. McPherson*   33

THE HUNTERS OF MOROWIE

In the early days of the Dreamtime when the northern Flinders Ranges were being created, two brothers went hunting in the rugged Mount Chambers Gorge. At Morowie Springs, near the eastern entrance, they caught an emu. After trussing it up for carrying, the elder brother placed it on his head.

The two continued their hunting until mid-day; but when they camped to prepare the emu for cooking, the flies, already troublesome, settled on its body in thousands. The brothers had just made the fire to drive away the pests, when a hot north wind sprang up.

It scattered the embers and burning sticks everywhere, lighting a bush-fire that raged so fiercely among the grass and low scrub that the hunters had to climb the steep sides of the gorge for safety. But the fire, still spreading, forced the men higher and higher up the cliffs until they were standing on the summit of a tall isolated peak.

But even there, the flames and smoke of the bush fire still surrounded them. So, to save themselves, the brothers flew up into the sky where they were changed into the brightest stars in the firmament, the Pointers of the Southern Cross.

27″ x 36″   *Mr Kenneth M. Gibb*   35

ULDANAMI, THE LITTLE MOTHER

It was a sad day for Uldanami, the little mother, when she heard that a bush-fire had driven her two sons into the sky. All of her other relatives having been dead for many years, her sons were the last on whom she could lavish her affection.

Lonely for human companionship, and unable to believe that her children were not on earth, Uldanami searched everywhere for them, her plaintive calls echoing and re-echoing among the rocky hills and steep gorges.

The spirits have now changed the little mother into the curlew, who still wanders at night, calling for her loved ones.

When, sitting beside their camp-fires, the aborigines hear that strange wailing call, they are reminded of the grief of Uldanami. It is then that the parents, pointing out the two bright stars in the southern sky, tell their children the story of how those stars were once the sons of the little mother, Uldanami.

Still mourning her loss, Uldanami believes that, if she calls loud enough and long enough, they will in time answer her call and return.

36″ x 27″   *Mr Kenneth M. Gibb*

THE ICE MAIDENS

Most aboriginal tribes have myths about the Pleiades, or, as we call them, the Seven Sisters. Some tribes believe that these stars are a flock of kangaroos, being eternally pursued by the dogs of the constellation of Orion; other tribes look upon them as a number of gum trees, under which the spirits of the dead shelter when travelling to their eternal home; and others believe that these stars are a family of young girls.

To the aborigines of north-eastern South Australia, the Seven Sisters, the Makara, are remarkable for their beauty. Their long, flaxen hair reaches down to their waists, and their bodies are covered with glistening icicles. These Makara, the wives of the men of Orion, disappear over the western horizon about an hour before the men. This gives them time to make a camp, and light a fire on which their husbands will cook the game they have speared during their daily journey across the sky.

During late winter when the Makara first appear in the eastern sky, the icicles falling from their bodies cover the earth beneath with a layer of frost. It is at these times that the older boys and girls go to the nearest spring, and, scraping the frost from the ground, rub it over their naked bodies.

This ritual makes the boys grow into strong and successful hunters, and the girls into beautiful women with large breasts. But they have to be most careful at these times for, should a beam of sunlight strike their bodies when covered with frost, they will always be weak and puny.

27" x 40"   *Miss Marcella Reale*   39

KONDOLE, THE WHALE

The mythology of Encounter Bay, in South Australia, tells how, at the time of the ceremonies, the day was so hot that the streams of perspiration pouring from the bodies of the actors created all the springs and watercourses in the neighbourhood.

As the performers had no means of providing light for the evening rituals, they invited Kondole hoping that he, being the sole owner of fire, would bring it with him. But being mean and disagreeable, Kondole simply hid the fire in the bush and arrived without it.

Enraged by his selfishness, the performers discussed several possible means of forcing him to bring his fire to the ceremonial grounds. But as Kondole was a large, powerful man, no one was brave enough to follow up any suggestion. Finally, one of the performers, completely losing his temper over Kondole's mean behaviour, crept up behind him and threw a spear that penetrated his skull.

Suddenly, the people of the ceremony were transformed into creatures. Some became kangaroos, some opossums, others the smaller creatures. Some rose into the air as birds, while others, entering the sea, were changed into fish in their many forms. Kondole, the largest of them all, became the whale who, ever since, has spouted water from the spear-wound in his head.

42" x 62"   *Whaler's Inn, Rosetta Bay*

41

THE FIRE TREE

The discovery of fire not only completely altered man's way of life, but set him apart from the rest of creation as nothing else could have done. A number of myths tell of its origin. Sometimes fire was given by a sky-dweller; often it was left by a lightning flash, or it was brought by a small bird after a long journey to a burning volcano.

A South Australian myth relates how a man, Kondole, hid his fire stick, rather than bring it with him to provide light for an evening's ceremony. When Kondole became a whale, another man, Tudrun, set out to find the precious fire stick. He had not searched for long when he saw a grass tree glowing with a strange light. This was Kondole's fire, which, escaping from its secret hiding place, had set alight the dry flower stem of the grass tree.

Ever since, when the aborigines need fire, they take a flower stem of the grass tree and rub it vigorously with a piece of harder wood. The friction causes Kondole's hidden fire to ignite the powdered wood-dust, and the aborigines have fire; fire to cook their food, fire to keep them warm, and fire to protect them from the dangerous spirits of the night.

27″ x 36″   *Mr and Mrs Feres Trabilsie*

THE FIRST BLACK SWANS

A group of women, the Wibalu, owned the only boomerangs in the world. The men of the surrounding tribes had often planned to take the weapons by force, but since the Wibalu used many powerful death chants to protect themselves, the men decided that it would be safer to acquire the boomerangs by guile.

So two of the tribe changed themselves into white swans, and flew to a waterhole near the women's camp. The men felt sure that when the swans flew overhead, the Wibalu, forgetting about their boomerangs, would rush away to see the strange birds.

The scheme worked perfectly. As soon as the camp was empty, the men, who had been hiding near by, seized the boomerangs and ran. The women, screaming with rage, rushed back to punish the thieves, but they had gone. The women then returned to attack the swans.

But the swans had flown to a lily-covered lagoon which, unknown to them, was the home of the eagles. Angry at the intrusion, the eagles picked up the swans in their powerful claws and carried them far south to a great desert. Savagely attacking the swans and tearing out most of their feathers, the eagles left their victims on the ground, bleeding and almost naked.

But a large flock of crows plucked feathers from their own bodies, letting them fall like a shower on the naked birds. "The eagles are our enemies too," they said, "our feathers will keep you warm, and help you to grow strong again."

Today, the black feathers of the crows cover almost every part of the swans. But the white feathers on the tips of their wings, and the blood on their beaks, still remain.

Birthplace of the Black Swan

Ainslie Roberts

27″ x 36″ *A.M.P. Society*

45

THE FIGHTING CLOUD-WOMEN

The Wibalu women were angry over the loss of their boomerangs. The exclusive possession of this weapon had given them a position of much power, and they were ashamed at the ease with which they had been tricked, turning them from people of importance to objects of ridicule.

The women could well imagine the roars of derisive laughter in the camp that would follow the account of their stupidity, and were fully conscious of the damage they had done to their boasted claims of superior intelligence.

Tempers were short and sharp in the camp of the Wibalus. Each woman was quick to accuse the other of rushing to see the white swans, and of forgetting that the men were always waiting for an opportunity to steal their boomerangs.

Storms of recrimination soon turned the whole camp into a melée of fighting women. At the height of this turmoil, the Wibalu were taken into the sky, where the blood from their many wounds stained the clouds a brilliant scarlet.

Today, when the aboriginal men see a vivid sunset they say to each other—"The Wibalu women are fighting again. Surely it's time they forgot their foolishness and their silly quarrelling."

27″ x 36″   *Private Collection, Tasmania*   47

THE MORNING STAR
AND HIS SONS

Wata-urdli had two sons who were unkind to him, and disobedient to the food-gathering laws of the tribe. Their behaviour was unpardonable, for those laws demanded that the younger men must always show their elders great respect and give to them the largest share of any game, the youths keeping for themselves the smaller and less desirable parts.

But the sons, not aware of the power of Wata-urdli, kept the full-grown kangaroos and gave the young ones to their father. Angry and disappointed over the actions of his sons, Wata-urdli planned to punish them. Taking the young kangaroos, he cut them in halves, and, by chanting magical songs, changed them into two flocks of full-sized kangaroos, one red, the other a slaty blue. Releasing the animals to feed on a near by plain, he pointed them out to his sons.

Idly rotating the shaft of his spear in the ground, the old man waited quietly until the youths had crept up and were about to throw their clubs at the kangaroos. Then, with a word of command, Wata-urdli changed his sons, their clubs, and the kangaroos into stars which slowly rose into the southern sky.

Satisfied with the punishment, Wata-urdli dropped through the hole he had made with his spear, and appeared on the other side of the world as the Morning Star, content in the knowledge that never again would he have to associate with his greedy, disobedient sons.

27″ x 36″   *Mr H. A. Badenoch*

THE ECHIDNA AND THE ROBIN

Echidna was a very old man who, living apart from his people, seldom left the shelter of his bark hut. No one knew where he collected his food. He was too old to hunt, yet in some way he prospered. Echidna actually lived on the flesh of young men whom he killed after coaxing them to his camp on some pretext. For a long time he had kept his secret, but, like all hidden things, it was finally revealed.

The aboriginal men, horrified when they found out what was happening, surrounded Echidna and wounded him so many times that his back was a bristling mass of spears, and his legs and arms were broken and distorted. Nunkito, the wife of Echidna, was so distressed when she heard about the punishment of her husband, that she gashed her scalp with a digging stick until the blood flowed down and stained her body. That is why, when Nunkito became a robin, she had a red breast.

Meanwhile, Echidna, though badly wounded, had crawled into a hollow log, where he stayed until his wounds were healed. When he came out his hands and feet were changed into strong, useful claws, and his legs, though badly distorted, were still able to carry him from place to place. But neither he, nor his wife, could pull the spears from his body.

One can often see Echidna, crawling slowly and awkwardly along the ground, his back bristling with spines, the spears of long ago. And should he be disturbed, Echidna, with his powerful digging claws, will quickly bury himself in the soft earth, for he still remembers the punishment he once received.

Thistles and Rocks

27″ x 36″   *Sir Robert Helpmann*

51

THE THEFT OF FIRE

A number of aboriginal myths describe how, in the long-distant past, attempts were made to destroy fire, so that man would again have to live in hardship and eternal darkness.

This myth from northern Australia describes how the crab-man, Unwala, the bat-man, Mulara, and the rainbow-man, Kanaula, having made a large catch of fish, arranged a corroboree to celebrate their good fortune. Unwala chanted the songs, Mulara led the dances and Kanaula blew the wooden trumpet, or didjeridoo.

But so many friends came to eat the fish and to take part in the dances that the corroboree continued well into the night. The singers and dancers were still enjoying themselves, but the rainbow-man, an irritable, belligerent old fellow, became tired of blowing the didjeridoo. So he made up his mind to stop the corroboree by jumping into the sea with the fire-stick which provided light for the dancers.

When Unwala saw what was happening he cast a spear, which, passing through the wrist of Kanaula, kept his hand above the water long enough for Mulara to grab the fire-stick, and throw it into a heap of pandanus leaves. The leaves, bursting into flame, saved fire for mankind. Kanaula then went into the sky and became the rainbow; the bat-man, Mulara, made his home in the trees, and Unwala, turning himself into a large crab, went to live in the mangrove swamps.

The Broken Flame

27″ x 36″   *F. Boyd Turner*   53

THE NINGAUIS

The Ningauis live in the dense mangrove swamps of an island, Imaluna, that lies off the northern coast of Australia. The Ningauis resemble the aborigines except that they are small people, about two feet high, with long hair and short feet. These little people gather their food only in the darkness, and as they do not know how to make fire, the crabs and shell-fish from the swamps, and the edible plants from the jungle, all have to be eaten raw.

Should an aboriginal go near to the homes of the Ningauis, one of them, calling out "Eeh", will cause the whole place to become pitch dark. And although the offender can bring the light back again by striking the trunk of a mangrove tree with a stick, the Ningauis, taking advantage of the darkness, will have disappeared. Therefore, no-one has ever seen a Ningaui, although the aborigines often hear them calling to each other.

When at night, the Ningauis perform their secret rituals and chant their songs, their home is as brightly lit as in the daytime. There are tales of hunters who, lured by the songs and light, have ventured into the swamps to find out what was happening. But as soon as the intruders were detected, the Ningauis made the swamp so dark, and the mangrove trees bend so closely together, that the strangers lost their way and died.

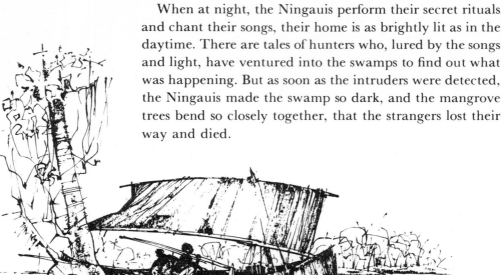

By Sudden Darkness of the Mangust   *Baeshe Roberts — 1941*

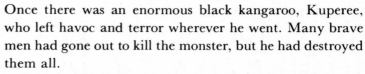

THE BLACK KANGAROO

Once there was an enormous black kangaroo, Kuperee, who left havoc and terror wherever he went. Many brave men had gone out to kill the monster, but he had destroyed them all.

Burdamuk, the leader of one tribe, owned a magical stone axe of great power. Yet, though he was too old to use the weapon against a kangaroo as large as Kuperee, Burdamuk refused to allow the axe out of his sight. For a long time there appeared to be no solution to the desperate situation until Indinya and Pilia, the two elder sons of the old man, finally persuaded their father to lend them the axe.

The brothers then searched for and found the empty camp of Kuperee, surrounded by the bones of his victims. Climbing into the dense foliage of a nearby myall tree, the brothers waited until Kuperee appeared. But when they threw their spears, the weapons, unable to penetrate the thick skin of the kangaroo, fell broken to the ground.

With a roar of fury, Kuperee charged into the trunk of the tree where the brothers were sheltering, hoping to uproot it. He had almost succeeded when Indinya, leaning outwards, struck the kangaroo such a heavy blow with the magical axe that it buried itself in his skull, killing him instantly.

Filled with joy at their success, Indinya and Pilia returned to tell their father and his people that they now could hunt without fear over the plains, or camp in peace beside the billabongs.

30" x 48"   *Chrysler Australia Limited*

JAPARA, THE MOON-MAN

In the long-ago Dreamtime, Purukupali, the great creator, savagely fought and severely wounded the moon-man, Japara, because he had been responsible for the death of Purukupali's son Jinini. Japara then made his home in the sky, still bearing on his face the scars from the wounds he had received.

Purukupali, frantic with grief over the death of his son, decreed that all living creatures, once dead, would never again come to life. But the moon-man partly escaped this decree, for, although he dies each month, his life is continuously renewed.

As soon as Japara re-appears, he greedily eats the flesh of the mangrove crabs in such huge quantities that, at the end of a fortnight he is filled to bursting point. But the continuous meals of this rich food finally make him so ill that once more he sickens and dies. The aborigines look upon the silvery crescent of the old moon as the skeleton of Japara, and the body of the old moon (seen by earth shine), as his spirit, Imunka.

During his nightly journeys across the sky, the moon-man, carrying a smaller torch than the sun-woman, Wuriupranali, follows her path. In early times, Japara returned to the east by a road just under the southern horizon. But a nest of hornets stung him so badly that he now uses the same underground passage as does the sun-woman, when she travels to the east to begin a new day.

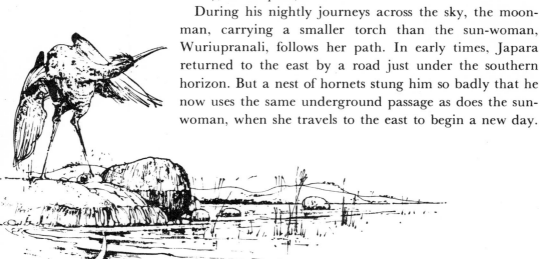

Rebirth of Tapera

36″ x 27″   *Mrs D. C. McCarthy*   59

WAMILI AND THE WARATAH

Wamili was a great hunter who, with the simple weapons of the aborigines, supplied his people with kangaroos, emus, bandicoots and other game. No one was more skilful than Wamili in tracking the creatures to their hiding places; and no other spear travelled as quickly or as accurately to its mark.

But although Wamili spent most of his time hunting, the delicacy he most liked was the honey of the scarlet waratah, and during the period of its blooming he enjoyed many hours collecting its sweetness.

One day a flash of lightning struck a nearby tree and hurled Wamili to the ground, where he lay unconscious until his companions found him some hours later. Although he appeared to be uninjured, it was soon evident that their famous hunter was totally blind.

No longer could he hunt, nor, when the trees were flowering, could his fingers distinguish the blossoms of the waratah from other flowers of the same size and shape. As some of them were poisonous and others filled with ants, not being able to distinguish between the blossoms caused Wamili much distress.

Kurita, the wife of Wamili, was so unhappy over the plight of her husband that she sought the help of the Kwinis, the tiny spirits of the bush, who agreed to make the pistils of waratah blossoms more rigid than those of the other flowers. And from that time Wamili, who then could find the waratah flowers by touch alone, searched with confidence for his favourite honey.

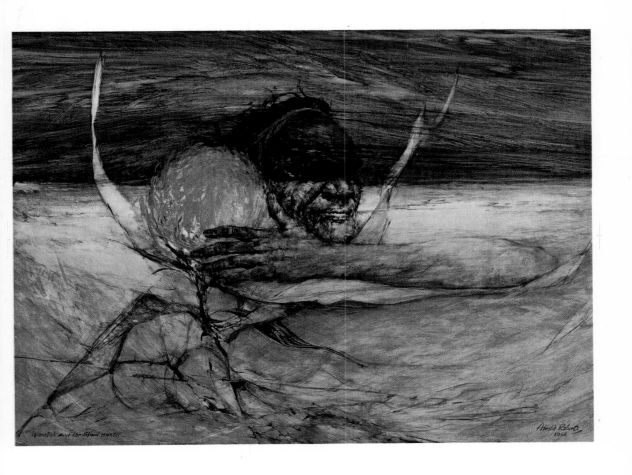

Wanatak and the Blind Hunter

Ainslie Roberts
1966

27" x 36"   *Mr Roger McKnight*

61

THE WATERS OF WINDULKA

From the beginning of time the task of food-gathering has occupied the greater part of the life of aboriginal men and women. This relentless, never-ending search has given rise to a number of myths which explain the creation of the topographical features of the countryside.

At one time during a severe drought, the bandicoot, Windulka, had to dig in so many places to get enough water to quench his thirst that the plain on which he lived was covered with burrows.

During the same period, the dingo, Banguruk, unable to find game in the arid hills, was forced to hunt on the plains. Seeing the bandicoot, the dingo immediately gave chase, but he was so weak with hunger that Windulka was able to escape into the dense scrub. But Banguruk, urged on by his craving for food, was relentless in his pursuit, and every time the bandicoot paused to rest, the dingo again attacked.

Finally, Windulka dug a burrow under a pile of boulders, knowing that Banguruk could not capture him in so confined a space. But when the bandicoot heard his enemy tearing at the rocks that blocked his way, Windulka, in his terror, dug deeper and deeper until, without warning, he released such a large spring of water that it flooded the whole plain, completely filling the burrows dug by Windulka.

Today these burrows are springs of cool, clear water. The land is covered with grass, and trees provide shade for the creatures and nesting places for the birds.

Dingo and Brumbies

27″ x 36″   *Mr Nigel Morgan*   63

KULPUNYA OF AYERS ROCK

At one time, when the hare-wallabies at Ayers Rock were initiating their youths, they received an invitation from the mulga-seed people of Kikingura, a mountain far away to the west, to attend one of their ceremonies, and to bring with them a parcel of eagle-down for body decorations. The hare-wallabies, annoyed by such an invitation when they were busy with their own rituals, sent a curt refusal. Instead of the eagle-down, they sent a parcel of white ash.

This insult made the mulga-seed tribesmen so angry that they decided to create a powerful spirit dingo, Kulpunya, who would kill all the people at Ayers Rock. So the spirit dingo was made with a mulga branch for a backbone, forked sticks for ears, the teeth of a marsupial mole and the tail of a bandicoot. But it was only after several days of secret rituals and the chanting of many lethal and malevolent songs, that the medicine men were able to bring Kulpunya to life with sufficient hatred and venom to carry out his task.

Meanwhile, the Ayers Rock people, not suspecting danger, were following their normal way of life. But an old Kingfisher-woman, Lunba, expecting an attack from the mulga-seed people, had built her camp high up on the rock so that she could watch for approaching enemies.

About mid-day when everyone else was asleep, Lunba saw Kulpunya in the distance. But although she gave the alarm, the spirit dingo destroyed most of the hare-wallabies before they were fully awake. There were, however, a number of initiates and their guardians who, on hearing Lunba's warning, fled to the east and escaped.

30″ x 40″   *Mr Rhys A. Roberts*

GECKO, THE RAIN-MAKER

A wide-spread myth describes huge reptilian creatures, sometimes lizards, but more generally snakes, each of whom lives in a waterhole belonging to a particular tribe. Local aborigines can drink from that waterhole without danger, though on occasions they may have to perform special rituals to please the mythical creature. On the other hand, should a stranger approach, the serpent will attack and injure his spirit so badly that, unless cured by a medicine man, the intruder will die.

On Groot Eylandt in the Gulf of Carpentaria, there is a gecko, Ipilya, about a hundred yards long, who lives in the Numarika swamp. This gecko is the creator of the thunderstorms and the monsoon rains.

When the rainy season is about to start, Ipilya, eating large quantities of water-grass and drinking a great deal of water from the swamp, squirts the mixture into the sky. The water quickly turns into thunderclouds, the grass binds them together, and in a short time the monsoon rains begin to fall, and the lightning strikes the ground.

It is then the gecko roars with the voice of thunder, delighted with his work and the benefits he has bestowed on the earth and its creatures. After the rainy season is over, Ipilya returns to his swamp where, except to punish intruders, he rests quietly until the next wet season is due.

Gecko the Rain Maker

27" x 36"   *Mr Andrew Tennant*

THE SALT LAKES OF KITI

The rich folk lore of the aborigines taught them not only the rules of tribal behaviour, but gave reasonable explanations about the creation of the world. This story tells how greed changed a rich, fertile plain into a desert of salt lakes.

Gumuduk was a tall, thin, medicine man, who belonged to the hills country. He owned a magical bone of such power that he could use it to make the rain fall in season, the trees bear much fruit, the animals increase, and the fish multiply. Because of such good fortune the hills people always had plenty of food.

However, the tribe that lived on the fertile plain below the Kiti range captured the medicine man and his bone, convinced that they, too, would in future have more food.

But instead of bringing them prosperity, the theft resulted in a calamity which totally destroyed their country. For the medicine man escaped, and was so angry over the indignity he had suffered that, plunging his magical bone into the ground, Gumuduk decreed that wherever he walked in the country of his enemies salt water would rise in his footsteps.

Those waters not only contaminated the rivers and lagoons, but completely inundated the tribal lands. And when these waters dried up, the whole area was changed to an inhospitable desert of salt lakes, useless to both the creatures and the aborigines.

The Bogman and the Salt Lakes

Ainslie Roberts
1966

27″ x 36″ , *Mrs Hubert Harvey*

THE BIRTH OF THE SUN

When the world was young, everyone had to search for food in the dim light of the moon, for there was no sun. Then came the time when the emu and the brolga, both of whom were sitting on a nest of eggs, had a violent argument over the excellence of their chicks. Finally the angry brolga ran to the nest of her rival and, taking one of her eggs, hurled it into the sky, where it shattered against a pile of sticks gathered by the sky-people.

The yolk of the egg, bursting into flame, caused such a huge fire that its light revealed, for the first time, the beauty of the world beneath. When the people in the sky saw this beauty, they decided that the inhabitants below should have day and night.

So every night the sky-people collected a pile of dry wood, ready to be set alight as soon as the morning star appeared. But this scheme was not successful, for if the day was cloudy, the star could not be seen, and no-one lit the fire. So the sky-people asked the kookaburra, who had a strong voice, to call them every morning.

When this bird's rollicking laughter is first heard, the fire in the sky throws out but little heat or light. By noon, when the whole pile of wood is burning, the heat is intense. Later, the fire begins to die down until, when the sun has set, only a few embers remain to colour the western sky.

It is a strict rule of the tribes that nobody may imitate the kookaburra's call, for such an act might so offend the bird that he would remain silent. Then darkness would again descend upon the earth and its inhabitants.

27″ x 36″   *Miss S. E. Welch*

BROLGA, THE DANCING GIRL

Brolga was the favourite of everyone in the tribe, for she was not only the merriest among them, but also their best dancer. The other women were content to beat the ground while the men danced, but Brolga must dance; the dances of her own creation as well as those she had seen. Her fame spread and many came to see her. Some also desired her in marriage, but she always rejected them.

An evil magician, Nonega, was most persistent in his attention, until the old men of the tribe told him that, because of his tribal relationship and his unpleasant personality, they would never allow Brolga to become his wife. "If I can't have her," snarled Nonega, "she'll never belong to anyone else." For already he had planned to change her from a girl into some creature.

One day, when Brolga was dancing by herself on an open plain near her camp, Nonega, chanting incantations from the centre of a whirlwind in which he was travelling, enveloped the girl in a dense cloud of dust. There was no sign of Brolga after the whirlwind had passed, but standing in her place was a tall, graceful bird, moving its wings in the same manner as the young dancer had moved her arms. When they saw the resemblance everyone called out "Brolga! Brolga!" The bird seemed to understand and, moving towards them, bowed and performed even more intricate dances than before.

From that time onward the aborigines have called that bird Brolga, and they tell their children how the beautiful girl was transformed into the equally beautiful grey bird which still dances on the flood plains of northern Australia.

27" x 36"   *Mr K. H. Kingsley*

73

THE BUNYIP

When the white men first came to Australia they were warned by the aborigines against the Bunyip, a strange creature which lived in a deep waterhole and destroyed everyone who camped nearby. Many early colonists, believing the story, never pitched their tents near a Bunyip hole and were careful not to unduly ruffle its surface when collecting water.

However, other settlers, with a more scientific turn of mind, endeavoured to gain some knowledge of this strange animal, thinking it possible that this aboriginal myth, so persistent and wide-spread, might contain some element of truth.

The Bunyip, under many names and forms, is known in all parts of Australia. The tribes in central Australia claim that the Wanambi, another form of the Bunyip, is an immense, highly coloured snake, often hundreds of feet long. It has a mane and a beard, lives in all permanent waterholes, and attacks any stranger that goes near its home. Some early drawings, made by the aborigines, show it as an emu-like creature.

Ainslie Roberts, after much reading and examination of old aboriginal drawings, has painted his own concept of a Bunyip. Although admittedly fanciful, and with humorous overtones, his Bunyip is likely to be as correct as any other. Nobody has ever seen a Bunyip, nobody ever will, for the creature exists only as a fantasy in the myths of the aborigines.

30″ x 48″   *Colonel Aubrey Gibson*

THE CALL OF TUKUMBINI

On Melville Island, at the close of the creation period, it was the man, Tukumbini, who instructed the mythical people how to create the aboriginal foods, and how to change themselves into the creatures, birds, fish and reptiles now belonging to the locality.

But first, Tukumbini taught them the rules of behaviour one to another; and, so that there would be peace in the tribe, the laws of marriage and social relationships. Tukumbini also laid down the periods of light and darkness that continue to determine the daily cycle.

When the first light of the sun-woman's torch shows in the eastern sky, it is the soft call of Tukumbini, now the yellow-faced honey-eater, that awakens the aborigines. The men go out hunting, and the women gather the vegetable foods from the forests and the swamps.

At noon, when the sun-woman makes the day uncomfortably hot by cooking the food she has gathered during the morning, the aborigines seek the shade of the jungle and remain there until the day is cooler. They then continue their food-gathering, returning to cook and eat their evening meal as the torch of the sun-woman sinks behind the western horizon.

Soon, darkness moves across the sky, the stars begin to show, and the twinkling fires of the men of the Milky Way span the heavens. In a short time the aborigines are asleep. Next morning they will again be wakened by Tukumbini, whose melodious call heralds yet another day.

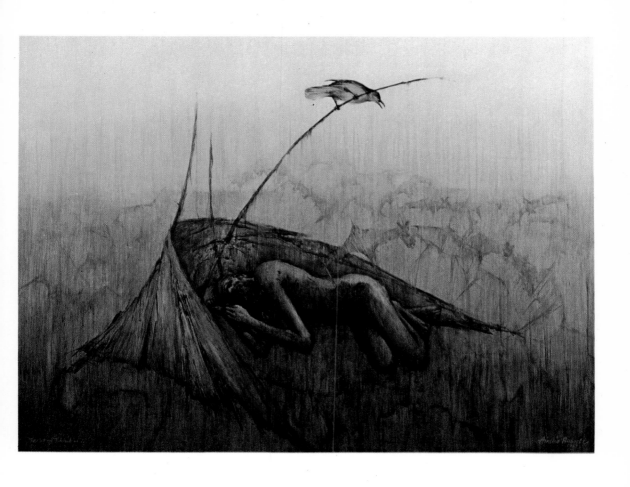

27" x 36"   *Mrs M. J. Roberts*   77

YURLUNGUR AND THE WAWALIK SISTERS

This myth is one of the most important in Arnhem Land, its ceremonies taking many weeks to perform. The aborigines believe that the Wawalik sisters came from a land far away to the east, and as they travelled they named the animals, the reptiles and the plants.

One day the women reached the Mirimina waterhole which, unknown to them, was the home of a dangerous serpent, Yurlungur. Here, the elder sister, knowing that she was about to give birth to a child, asked the younger to prepare a bark hut where she could shelter. The younger sister had just completed the task when a son was born.

Yurlungur, hearing the women moving above him, became angry over their intrusion. Stirring the water into a maelstrom, he rose to the surface and, accompanied by roars of thunder and flashes of lightning, approached the camp of the two sisters. Terrified, they chanted their most powerful songs to frighten Yurlungur away, but were unsuccessful.

In desperation, the women crept into their bark hut and blocked the openings with branches and grass. But the enraged serpent, pushing these obstructions aside without difficulty, swallowed first the younger, then the elder Wawalik sister and finally, her son. Yurlungur then retired to the seclusion of the Mirimina waterhole, where he has lived ever since.

27″ x 36″   *Mr E. J. Barker*   79